# Special Edition Self-Help Handbook

## 365 Collector Gold Series

@Poetic Author

STEVEN ALLEN GRAHAM

PAGE PUBLISHING
Conneaut Lake, PA

First originally published by Page Publishing 2024

ISBN 979-8-89315-278-4 (pbk)
ISBN 979-8-89315-323-1 (digital)

Printed in the United States of America

# Contents

# Rehab Demo: Flip Side Recovery

Sitting, falling,
Striving,
But stalling,
Not asking,
No answer,
Separated,
Heading for disaster.
Failing to return to abstinence,
Distorted,
Striking out,
Not the answer,
Go nowhere, relapse,
Need another chapter.
Start over,
Stand up,
Give the drugs and alcohol up,
You'll have some luck,
Come on, focus,
You need the buck.
Looking forward to reunite,
Be heard,
No fright,
Enhance,
Take this choice,
You'll be successful,
Channel your voice.
Stand, gain,
No one to blame,
Take initiative, reframe,
Dodge the next storm,
Speaking in abstinence,
Summary,
Success again,
Now you have the resistance…

# Perfect Resolution

## Poetic-Cognitive Spectrum/Advanced Semantics

PREVAILING POETIC STRATEGY... When cognitive decision ability brought us here, who would not cheer? Be competent my consumer; no carelessness to adhere. Clients want perfection, while others with objection, still hold on to overgraded sophisticated inception. Know this within... Subjects do this to contend; disorganized thoughts are not pretend... Again over again consumers defend; unfiltered processing. In the heart awaits an amend. Now let's subdue, past what we once knew; thus clients progress from old to new... This may be you, environment-friendly too. See yourself through this; subjects set your tasks to this... I prioritize never one consumer bestow; for disorganized thoughts are not control. Now when clients stand up, to make a resolution. I state this fact of nonfiction solution... Subjects set your mind to it: step 1—AWARENESS, step 2—IDENTIFY, step 3—APPRAISAL, step 4—SIGNIFICANCE, step 5—MAGNITUDE, step 6—DECISIONS... Make this improvement like; there's nothing to it. Defend your primary objective. Implement resolution affirmation. Decline to make unjust altercations next. It is not difficult, nor even complex. This provision given through time, may refine and subdue us. Consumer stick to this... Justify yourself; stand up and just do this... PREVAILING POETIC STRATEGY...When life came to adhere... PROGRESSIVE SENSIBLE SOLUTION...

# Alcohol Perpetrator & Scenario

Typical alcoholic… codependent;
Playing for keeps? What's for real?
Alcohol, seems every other day,
Perhaps to judge, perhaps to feel.
What are pending pros and cons?
Alcohol helps me cope with my life,
Alcohol helps me in social stride.
Alcohol brings me small lies,
Alcohol brings me tall strife.
Alcohol, penetrating, progressive,
Alcohol demonstrating, excessive.
To say the most, less to least,
Alcohol gives me what I need.
Think I'm big, think I'm strong,
Although in the end I am weak.
Falling down, I'm coming down,
Alcohol again, back on the street.
Is codependent the way to go?
Or am I just helpless and weak?
This to life, therefore to weigh;
Is it so good? Some say pathetic.
Someday I might really regret it.
Typical alcoholic… codependent;
Playing for keeps? What's for real?
Alcohol seems every other day,
Subject to judge, subject to feel…

# Crazy Groundhog

Today's crazy groundhog, crazy or what?
He is one incognito fellow alright,
He comes out to check the weather.
He checks for a beam of sunlight,
Several community folks seem to gather.
Is crazy groundhog sophisticated enough?
We hope that today he's got it together.
For him overcast may seem to be tough,
Everyone look, he's now predicting the weather.
Oh no, he now fell down, that's rough.
Look he's now standing up, he's got it together,
He's seeing sun and shadow, that's powerful stuff.
Look, I guess we don't need someone better,
Test proved crazy groundhog confident enough.
Reformed hog predicts six weeks of bad weather,
Today's crazy groundhog, crazy or what?

# Addiction & Conduct Remission

Now foreseeing abstinence,
In turn to good conduct.
By admitting the problems,
My life can turn around…good times!
No more drug addictions,
Currently a big challenge.
Emotions always changing,
One can't be in constant denial.
Too deprived to go on,
Too impulsive to see,
Too much anxiety…not healthy!
Too much anger remaining,
One can't keep this within.
By admitting the problems,
I can move on to see.
By letting go and letting God,
I'll have another shot at being me.
Now foreseeing abstinence,
In turn to good conduct.
God's credited for our best…good luck!

# Valentine for You

I would if I could,
What is the word?
Valentine for you.
I like you to know,
I won't falsely bestow,
From what I have for you.
I might if I should,
I would if I could,
Give this message to you.
What is the word?
Haven't you heard?
Valentine for you.
Don't you forget,
The poem that you get,
And what I feel for you.
What is the word?
Haven't you heard?
Valentine for you!

# Yet to Be

What is yet to be?
How are you today?
By the looks of things,
I would like to say,
Hint, hint, this says relationship.
If you're the one,
Knowing you,
Knowing me,
Given a chance,
We're yet to be.
What is yet to be?
How are you today?
Friendship with you,
Friendship with me,
Given a chance,
We're yet to be.
What is yet to be?
How are you today?
Hint, hint, knowing you, and me,
Trusting all our feelings see,
With friendship,
These relationships,
What is yet to be!

# Presidents' Day

The US greatly appreciates Presidents' Day;
In honor of all their performance,
Substantial responsibilities each day.
Such wisdom, ambition, and dedication,
Progressing the people and what they say.
Giving assurance, with direction to subsidize.
The US greatly appreciates Presidents' Day…

# Poetic Justice:
# America Progressive United

America free, proud, alive,
One in together we stride.

Starting out so tall,
With peace and justice for all.

The land we know is won,
You're invited to come.

For our nation will never condemn,
All but to any, newcomers or their kin.

Once in and all legal,
You'll progress to see justice.

America free, proud, alive,
One in together we stride…

# St. Patrick's Green

It's St. Patrick's Day,
I have a nice plan,
Green is the color,
It's in high demand.
A whole lot of green,
Or just a touch,
Not to be mean,
But you're not the such.
You know the saying,
It calls for a pinch,
Don't get mad,
It's rather a cinch.
Maybe next year,
You'll keep in mind,
When wearing green,
We'll treat you fine.
Lucky is,
As lucky does,
Green is the color,
It's all because,
You need to have your way,
It's St. Patrick's Day…

# Progressional Marriage

Precedingly submissive… Family tree submitted.

Thy flirt… Thy flaunt… Thy tease… Thy taunt, How charming thy want? IN LOVE THAT IS WELL. Thy talk-we touch… They are staring too much! Thy kiss… Thy touch… Thy promised to hush. HAVING FRIENDS TURN TO ROMANCE… Thy progressively; thee romance.

IN LOVE THAT IS WELL… Thy good things… In good time… Thy looking so fine… Thy backed by his all… Committed to love where thy fall. IN LOVE THAT IS WELL… PROMISE RING WHERE HE STOOD. She nudged that he definitely could. WHAT NOW? On thy knee… GOD GIVEN TO THEE. Thy love for an eternity it shall be to thee. How nifty proclaimed; what an empowering thing… THY VOW… She gleams… THEE PROPOSED GIVING THY RING; Thy veil it lifted… Thy kiss… Thy love then drifted thee spirits forever uplifted. Thy sparkling glass red wine; very much looking so fine. Momentarily and proceedingly forever perfectly entwined.

Family tree submitted… Predicted submissive…

# Glistening Streets of Gold

The chosen elementary withstanding configuration…
Uprising the youth age seeing effortlessly starred in humanity…
Retrograded for shiny and new…
Stargazing yet seeing through the mindfulness…
A perfect being…
All beyond the star-gate of adulthood…
Looking back…
The midst…
A new dawn…
Seeking knowledge…
Glimpsing…
Yet preferred super-faces…

The perfect destiny.

# God & I

God I'll try,
Just you and I,
I think you know why,
For your love will,
Forever tie,
The bond we carry.
Unbreakable,
Everlasting,
Surpassable,
Breathtaking,
My light,
My shield,
In the light,
Or any field.
Bound close,
And yet so far,
Everlasting,
And by far,
Oh, what a tie,
God I'll try,
Just you and I…

# Easter Egg Hunt

We are painting the eggs,
With wage to the hunt,
Some for the toddlers,
That is what we want.
Ages six and up,
Surely will find enough.
They will fill their baskets,
It might be tough.
They are eager for the count,
Even more for the buck,
Cashing the eggs in,
All that good stuff.
Now seeing toddlers hush,
From a frown to a grin,
They are so special,
Let's see, what did they win?
There are ages six and up,
Standing sharing their luck,
Looks like several eggs found,
Let's count them all up.
From a dime to a dollar,
To a five to a ten.
Likely jumping and shouting,
Let's hide all the eggs,
Let's do it all again!

# Happy Emotion

What makes the day?
What steers us to joy?
What makes me happy?
Birthdays, candles, cake.
Another year of age,
Not just getting older,
Another year I won.
Friends are always by me,
Another yet to come,
When we're all together,
It creates lots of fun.
Don't forget the smiling,
Attitudes we have one.
All those to favor,
All who are yet to come.
What makes the day?
What steers us to joy?
Things that make me happy,
And great and full of joy!

# Blue-Collar Mother

Is a good day…blue-collar mother.
Working a trade…blue-collar mother.
Bring a trace…blue-collar mother.
Is a good way…blue-collar mother.
Bills are paid…blue-collar mother.
Be not dismayed…blue-collar mother.
Smile my face…blue-collar mother.
Player be ace…blue-collar mother.
Everyone so say…blue-collar mother.
Do not hesitate…blue-collar mother.
Party with her…blue-collar mother!

# Running Around About

Are you coming around?
Are you going to come about?
Can you hear me?
Enough of the running about.
Tell me if you want to know me,
Give me a sign.
Tell me if I should know you.
I'll talk, are you coming around?
Show me a nod, a smile,
I want to catch your style.
A ship without a dock,
Will never rest.
Enough of the running about.
This is not enough.
Give me a sign,
I need to feel what's in your mind.
Are you coming around?
Are you going to come about?
Can you hear me?
Enough of the running about…

# Memorial Day Tribute

With now to be laid to rest;
We knew them at their best.
Must give sympathetic confess,
Another day had been request,
But in this we are at rest.
Transition we are not to be less;
The gift of life is just a test,
Per Judgment Day is our quest.
Thus progressing us to heaven.
In this we are truly blessed,
Amen; for God is love always…

# Prime Negotiation & Silver Dollar

Peace…due prime negotiation;
Rather in by choice; demonstrate.
When wrong shall I compensate,
All is within to illustrate,
From which is fact or fiction.
Your opinion versus myself.
Setting aside all but principle.
Organized, prompt, visible,
To always be thought various.
Knowing the key to wisdom,
Being versatile per all topics.
Initially pertaining to following;
In which to define; perception.
To what sequence of thought.
From what which brings choice.
Bringing forth to see action.
Thus to decide prediction.
Now need not manipulate;
Submit, study, incorporate,
Due to justly see…negotiate;
Yet not to hesitate; fail this,
Perhaps toss the silver dollar…

# Blue-Collar Father

Is a God day…blue-collar father.
Working a trade…blue-collar father.
Bring a trace…blue-collar father.
Is a good way…blue-collar father.
Bills are paid…blue-collar father.
Be not dismayed…blue-collar father.
Smile my face…blue-collar father.
Player be ace…blue-collar father.
Everyone so say…blue-collar father.
Do not hesitate…blue-collar father.
Party with me…blue-collar father!

# Addiction Outcast & Control

Likely grieving loss of power,
Thus lack of confidence.
Subject high-risk abuser.
Turning this into a positive,
Rehabilitation process due.
Finding a means of progress;
Should be one with God.
Promptly your wrongs.
Begin a twelve-step program,
Admit all your problems,
Honestly working the steps,
Excelling the step power,
Beginning daily abstinence.
Subdue to first things first,
Taking one day at a time,
Role modeling easy does it.
Subject being confident;
Implementing an excellence,
Pertaining to new business,
Regaining power and control…

# Patriots Day & Freedom

Freedom, Glory, Red, White, and Blue;
Flags on so really high. All standing
so proudly too; Fact shown proudly
nigh. Look town's best fireworks
stand; number 1 choice firecrackers here.
Everyone's stuck such high demand;
Most traditional July 4 cheer.
Not least snakes and ladyfingers;
Assorted Black Cats too. Please
Smoke still lingers. Popsicles, red,
white, and blue. Conspicuous, not
peculiar… I am still stalling for
you. Everyone's seeking display
time; at most now at the park.
Gratitude awesome summertime,
Going from daylight till dark.
Night show has been unique;
Still standing so proudly too.
Winding down, feeling complete;
Freedom, Glory, Red, White, and Blue…

# Falling Off the Wagon

Mighty high and tall,
Not too big, not too small,
Once on the right track,
They'll give me the back.
Are you not here?
It's so wrong,
The thrill is not strong,
Not for today,
Not for tomorrow,
With these addictions comes only sorrow.
Come one,
Come all,
Come now,
Turn the next page,
Start the new chapter,
Give the stuff up,
It's all that will matter,
You'll hear or see no more negative chatter.
Once and for all,
Back on the wagon,
No longer hungry, lonely, tired, or unacceptable,
Just doing what's right,
That's what's respectable.
They're for staying on track,
It will be your final back…

# Labor Day Blues

Don't laugh, I'm stuck just a working away.
I can't do the throw-down barbeque.
High functional working class I must say;
Catch me on another day would be your cue.
Mandatory punching the clock this day.
Although while working my troubles are few,
My family will never forgive me this day.
Summary, I'm blue not there grilling with you.
Don't laugh, I'm stuck just a working away…

# Destiny of Light

Where there is a will,
There is a way.
Where there is hope,
Our thoughts should not astray.

Where there is attraction,
There is desire.
Where love is not true,
We still have each other.

Where there is a touch,
There is giving.
Where we receive,
Our kindness is remembered.

Where there is one with God,
There is strength.
Where there is Christ,
We have love and forgiveness…

# Columbus Day:
# America We Stand

America is found with pride,
Watch us as we stride.
Starting out by the English;
He made history as we see it.
For our nation has been claimed.
The proof will always remain,
Time has been on our side.
We will always state amen;
Watch this America we stand…

In reference; in the USA, many states and localities now also observing
Indigenous Peoples' & International Indigenous Peoples Day.

# Valid Perception

You see it,
You feel it,
You say it,
You be it.

You bring it,
You thrill it,
You reason it,
You deal it.

It is real,
It is solid,
It is light,
It is to seek.

It is just,
It is for you,
It is a must,
It is sleek.

We can look,
We can take,
We can give,
We can make.

We can see it,
We can reach,
We can love,
We can teach!

# Halloween-Scare Analogy

See for the night is the night; thus
See for the day is the day; thus
For it is likely just choice per conduct,
For now don't you cry, keep faith.
See for the black is the black; thus
See for the white is the white; thus
For it is likely just choice per conduct,
For now don't you cry, keep faith.
See for the bad is the bad; thus
See for the good is the good; thus
For it is likely just choice per conduct,
For now don't you cry, keep faith.
See for when you're feeling scared;
See for feeling night, black, or bad.
For pray you have a day, white, and good,
For God's light shall overcome per subject!

# Christian Soldier

Christian soldier,
Born of God,
Follower of Christ.
Prompt to rely,
In thy word,
At thy light,
With thy shield.
I won't procrastinate,
I don't deny,
I am heard.
All my might,
Unto God's will.
Proud to state,
Christian soldier…

# Veterans Day

Complementary notice to United States veterans;
We give a big tip to the hat per veteran.
The United States relies on its skilled military.
Our heroes control all military resources,
Giving their best performance; no regrets.
Signing their lives over to achieve; and excel;
Serving the United States for freedom; and independence.
Implementing everything the military offers.
Complementary notice to United States veterans…

# Two-Way & Multicommunication

Two-way or multicommunication is subject.
In many conversations,
There must be some concentration,
If one exceeds the duration,
Of which one can solve,
With or without a stipulation,
In various situations.
Two-way or multicommunication is subject.
So hear me out,
Memorize these instructions.
Try to stand strong,
When you speak, read, or listen.
Observe, speak when necessary,
Primarily to topic.
Read a lot,
But know when to stop.
Get the point,
Pass it on,
Channel in, and listen strong.
You'll do fine,
Pertain to business.
Remember your objectives and missions.
Subdue to all this,
Just like I tell you,
But don't forget this.
Two-way or multicommunication is subject.
So submit at any given location,
Within the duration,
Of every population,
For general or progressive justification…

# Thanksgiving Day Harvest

It's Thanksgiving Day Harvest,
The gardens are all in.
Big count on frozen ears of corn.
There are several pounds of potatoes in baskets,
The cardboard is mangled and torn.
There are pie pumpkins and gourds,
With some squash in bushels,
Stored and still to be washed.
The bushel baskets are faded and worn.
There are cases of canned tomatoes,
With dozens of jars of pickled okra,
With pint-size jars of pickled beets,
You know that will be quite a treat.
There are cases of canned green beans,
With several pints of sweet potatoes, carrots,
Also some quarts of sweet peas,
It's all stocked down in the cellar.
There are large quantities of eggs in the fridge.
There are a couple of Tom Gobblers,
Along with some frozen hens,
They're all from up on the ridge.
We have some butchered swine,
It's tasty and mighty fine,
We have flour in the bin.
You know there were very high yields,
From all the gardens and fields,
We are obviously ready for the kin.
We have our big leaf table set,
Many people are invited without regret.
On a year like this, all can't resist,
I cannot ever forget this day,
It's Thanksgiving Day Harvest…

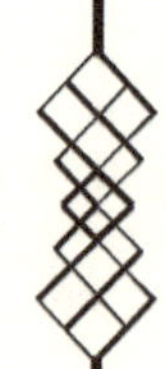

# Recovery & Incentive Poem

Now with my abstinence,
By saying no,
I'll be free from addictions,
It sounds like a go.
No more ineffective request,
Looks like success,
Now I'll finally be at best.
Here I now go,
Now everyone may know,
Never again will I falsely bestow,
From my religion, job, anyone, or anything.
I think you should know you're not to blame.
I will plan for this stand,
It is a good plan,
Relapse prevention is high demand.
First things first,
One day at a time,
Easy does it,
I'm doing fine.
When I include my higher power,
I will thrive,
Now when I work it will be with pride.
My opportunity is finally at best,
My abstinence is in,
And I'm high request...

# Christmas Cheer & Jesus

IT'S ALL ABOUT JESUS. He is the one. The day is Christmas Jesus Christ has come. All through the times. We didn't stop believing. Christmas carols chime. Savior's thoughts are retrieving. Jesus Christ has come. The reason Christmas time is here. Unwrapped gifts express giving. Presents open with cheer. Remembering the special north star. That marked his birth. How he came to heal others. That's what he is worth. Far and close near and far. Jesus Christ is most. For our thoughts truly acquire. Christmas has come true. So never stop believing. What Jesus Christ can do at the time of the season. When honoring Jesus. All surely won't miss this. For when it comes to Christmas. THE TOPIC IS JESUS…

# About the Author

The format of this book is designed by state-of-the-art hands-on technology.

Educated to a high standard self-help competitor.

Composition including innovation intended; fun positive purposes only.

Present this literature of my best work in regard to the consumer.